nature's friends

Bees

by Ann Heinrichs

Content Adviser: Janann Jenner, Ph.D.

Science Adviser: Terrence E. Young Jr., M.Ed., M.L.S., Jefferson Parish (La.) Public Schools

Reading Adviser: Dr. Linda D. Labbo, Department of Reading Education, College of Education, The University of Georgia

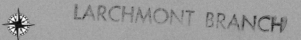

COMPASS POINT BOOKS
MINNEAPOLIS, MINNESOTA

Compass Point Books
3722 West 50th Street, #115
Minneapolis, MN 55410

Visit Compass Point Books on the Internet at *www.compasspointbooks.com*
or e-mail your request to *custserv@compasspointbooks.com*

Editors: E. Russell Primm and Emily J. Dolbear
Photo Researchers: Svetlana Zhurkina and Jo Miller
Photo Selector: Linda S. Koutris
Designer: The Design Lab

Library of Congress Cataloging-in-Publication Data

Heinrichs, Ann.
   Bees / by Ann Heinrichs.
     p. cm. — (Nature's friends)
   Includes bibliographical references (p.).
   Summary: Introduces distinguishing characteristics, life cycles, and different types of bees.
   ISBN 0-7565-0165-2 (hardcover)
   1. Bees—Juvenile literature. [1. Bees.] I. Title. II. Series: Heinrichs, Ann. Nature's friends.
  QL565.2 .H45 2002
  595.79'9—dc21   2001004972

Table of Contents

Bees Are Busy!

Buzz, buzz, buzz! Bees are busy all day long. They go from flower to flower. They collect what they need to make honey and **wax.** Bees eat the honey. They build their nests with the wax.

People love to eat honey, too. Honey was the first dessert in history! People also make many useful things from beeswax.

◀ *A bumblebee lands on a flower.*

Kinds of Bees

Bees live all over the world—almost. No bees live near the North Pole or the South Pole. There are many kinds of bees. Some live alone. Others live in big family groups, or colonies. These are called social bees.

Thousands of bees may live in one colony. Their nest is called a beehive. Most bees in our gardens are honeybees or bumblebees. They are social bees.

A huge group of bees on a tree ▶

The Body of a Bee

A bee has three main body parts—the head, the **thorax,** and the abdomen. On the head are five eyes. Three of these eyes are very small. The other two are huge **compound eyes.** Bees can see shapes and some colors. But colors look different to bees than they look to us.

Bees have a mouth with a long tongue. The tongue is like a long tube. Bees smell with their antennae, or feelers.

On its thorax, a bee has four wings and six legs. In the bee's abdomen are two stomachs. One is a regular stomach. The other is called a honey stomach. At the end of the bee's body is a stinger.

◀ *The bee's body has three main parts.*

Bees Built for Work

Bees are fuzzy with hair all over their bodies. Pollen from flowers sticks to the hairs. The golden grains of pollen help flowers make seeds. The pollen is also food for the bees. A bee's two back legs have pollen baskets.

A bee's tongue is shaped like a long tube. It sucks a sweet juice called **nectar** from flowers. Bees make honey with the nectar. They eat the honey and make it into wax.

Pollen catches in the bee's hair. ▶

At Home in a Honey Tree

Bees build their hives in hollow places. Hollow trees are good places for hives. Bees cover the inside of the hive with a honeycomb made of wax. The honeycomb has many six-sided spaces called cells. Inside each cell is a bee egg, a young bee, or honey.

Animals love honey, just as many people do. Sometimes a bear tries to get honey from a beehive. Guard bees try to scare the bear away.

◄ *Some bees live in hollowed out logs.*

Life in a Beehive

Every hive has a queen bee. She is the mother of every bee in her colony! Her only job is to lay eggs. Out of each egg comes a **larva.** It grows into a **pupa** and then into an adult bee.

Most bees grow up to be worker bees. All workers are females. They build the honeycomb and collect nectar and pollen. Then they make honey and wax. They feed the other bees, too. Workers can make a special food called royal jelly. A larva that is fed royal jelly becomes a queen.

A few bees are males, called drones. Their job is to **mate** with the queen. Then she can lay eggs.

The large queen bee (center) is surrounded by smaller worker bees. ▶

The Honey Dance

Some bees are food **scouts.** They fly around and find places where flowers grow. Then they come back and tell the other bees. They tell the story by dancing a honey dance.

A honey dance is an awesome sight! The scout dances in a figure eight. It wiggles its tail as it dances. The figure eight points to the left or right of the sun. This tells the bees where the flowers are. Dancing faster means the flowers are nearby. A slower dance means they are farther away.

◀ *A honey dance*

Making Honey and Wax

A bee collects nectar from a flower. It stores the nectar in its honey stomach. Then it flies back to the hive. It spits the nectar out into the honeycomb. Soon the nectar changes to honey.

To make wax, a bee eats honey. Inside the bee's body, the honey changes to wax. Then the wax oozes out of its body. The bee uses the wax to build or repair the honeycomb.

A drone uses wax to cover a cell of honeycomb. ▶

Beekeeping

People have kept honey bees for thousands of years. They liked having honey nearby.

Today, beekeepers keep bees for their honey and wax. They also keep them to help farmers spread pollen for their crops. Beekeepers wear special clothes to avoid stings. Some wear hats with veils and heavy gloves.

Many people keep bees as a hobby. They like to watch how bees live and work together.

◀ *A beekeeper gets ready to collect honey from a hive.*

When a Bee Stings

Bees are not looking for someone to sting. They sting only when they think they are in danger.

When a bee stings, it leaves its stinger in its victim. Soon that bee dies. The stinger has venom, or poison, inside.

A bee sting feels like a pinprick. The spot may itch and swell up. A few people get sick from a sting. They may need special medicines for bee stings.

The area around a bee sting becomes quite red. ▶

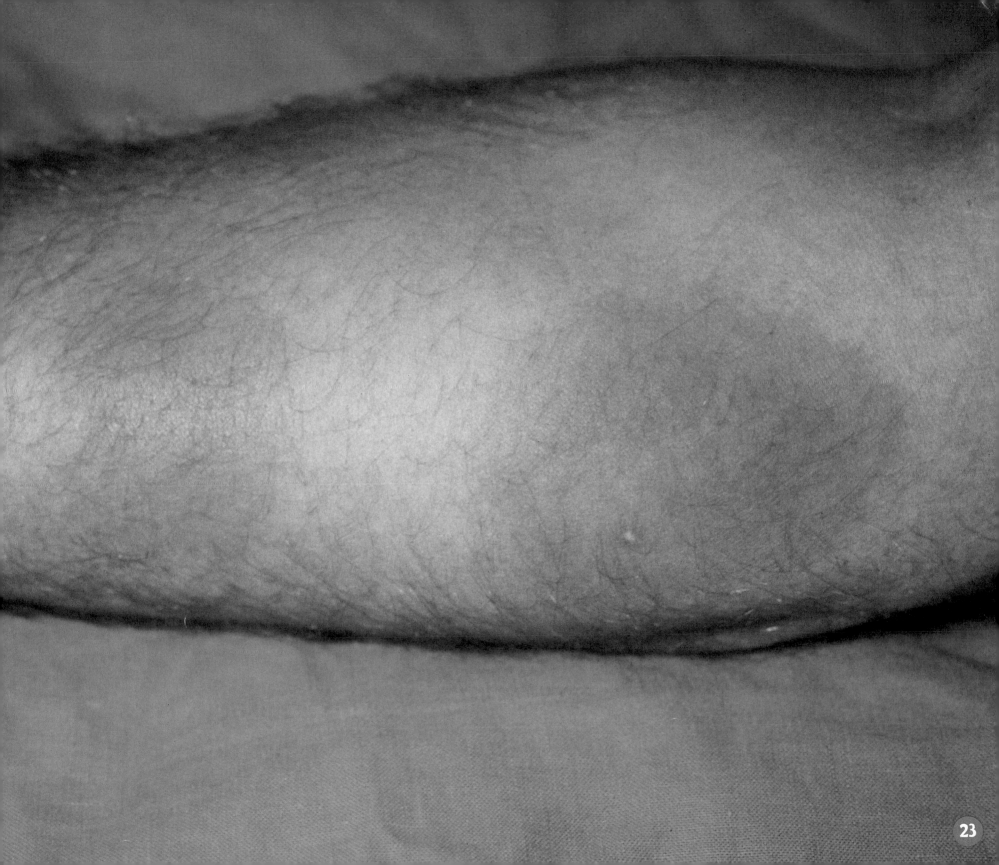

Killer Bees!

Scientists in South America developed a new kind of bee. They believed it would produce more honey. First they got some bees from Africa. Then they mated those bees with local bees. The new bees were called Africanized honeybees. Some of these bees escaped and flew north. In 1990, they reached the southern United States.

These bees are sometimes called killer bees. They have a bad temper, and their sting can be very dangerous. Killer bees have killed some people's pets and cattle. But they rarely kill people.

◀ *Africanized bees are sometimes called killer bees.*

Bees Are Our Friends

Bees are good friends. They give humans honey to eat. Their wax is made into many things. Candles, crayons, and lipstick are all made from beeswax.

Bees help farmers, too. They carry pollen from one flower to another. This helps the crops make fruit and seeds. Many fruit trees cannot make fruit without the help of bees.

Next time you use crayons or eat honey, think of the busy bees. They work hard for all of us!

Many things are made from beeswax and honey. ▶

Glossary

compound eyes—eyes that are made up of many tiny eyes

larva—the wormlike form an insect takes after hatching from an egg and before becoming a pupa

mate—to join together to produce young

nectar—a sweet liquid produced by plants

pupa—the form an insect takes after being a larva and before becoming an adult

scouts—members of a group who are sent out to find something and bring information back to the group

thorax—the middle part of an insect's body

wax—a yellow, sticky substance made by bees

Let's Look at Bees

Class: Insecta
Order: Hymenoptera
Family: Apidae

Range: Honeybees are found on all continents except Antarctica. They live in open woodlands, forests, and grasslands.

Life span: Queen bees can live from one to three years. Drones and workers live only for about five weeks.

Life stages: All the eggs in a hive are laid by the queen. They hatch in three days.

Food: Honeybees are herbivores. Herbivores are creatures that eat things that come from plants. Honeybees eat nectar and honey. Their larvae eat pollen and royal jelly—a special food made by worker bees.

Did You Know?

A queen bee can lay up to 1,500 eggs a day. These 1,500 eggs weigh as much as the bee!

A queen bee has a curved stinger. She can sting many times without hurting herself. The stingers of worker bees are straight and barbed. This means they have many smaller sharp edges that stick out all over them. When a worker bee stings someone, its stinger gets stuck in the creature's flesh. When the bee tries to get away, the organs inside its body get torn and the bee dies.

One of the jobs of a worker bee is to be sure the nest or hive doesn't get too hot. If it does, a whole group of worker bees fans its wings to cool off the hive.

In cold weather, the workers all gather around the nursery so their body heat will keep the baby bees warm.

One worker bee produces about one-twelfth of a teaspoon of honey in its lifetime.

Junior Entomologists

Entomologists are scientists who study insects. You can be an entomologist, too! Try this simple experiment. You will need a notebook, a pen or pencil, a watch, and a pair of binoculars. Find a place with several different kinds of flowers. Choose three different types of flowers to observe. Write down the name or a description of each type of flower in a notebook. Then sit down quietly and watch one kind of flower at a time. Use your binoculars to see the flowers and bees close up. Don't get too close. Also be careful to sit still and not disturb the bees! Every time a bee visits a flower, make a mark next to its name in your notebook.

**After observing each kind of flower for five minutes,
try to answer these questions:**
How many bees visited each type of flower?
Do you think one of the flowers was a favorite of bees?
    Why or why not?
If there was a favorite type of flower, why do you think it was the favorite?
What did the bees you saw look like?
What parts of the flower did the bee land on?
Draw a picture of a bee.

Want to Know More?

AT THE LIBRARY

Crewe, Sabrina. *The Bee.* Austin, Tex.: Raintree/Steck-Vaughn, 1997.

Gibbons, Gail. *The Honey Makers.* New York: William Morrow, 1997.

Schaefer, Lola M. *Honey Bees and Hives.* Mankato, Minn.: Pebble Books, 2000.

ON THE WEB

Enter the Hive

http://wnet.org/nature/alienempire/multimedia/hive.html

To enter a virtual beehive and watch what goes on

Tales from the Hive

http://www.pbs.org/wgbh/nova/bees/

For an inside look at beehives and how bees live

THROUGH THE MAIL

Smithsonian Institution

Office of Education

National Museum of Natural History

Constitution Avenue and 10th Street, N.W.

Washington, DC 20560

202/357-2700

ON THE ROAD

The Philadelphia Insectarium

8046 Frankford Avenue

Philadelphia, PA 19136

215/338-3000

To watch a working beehive in this all-bug museum

Smithsonian Institution

National Zoological Park

Pollinarium and Vanishing

Pollinators Exhibit

Washington, DC 20008

202/673-4717

For close-up encounters and educational exhibits on bees and other pollinators

Index

About the Author: Ann Heinrichs grew up in Fort Smith, Arkansas. She began playing the piano at age three and thought she would grow up to be a pianist. Instead, she became a writer. Now she has written more than fifty books for children and young adults. Several of her books have won national awards. Ms. Heinrichs now lives in Chicago, Illinois. She enjoys martial arts and traveling to faraway countries.